Call of the
LOON

Call of the
LOON

David C. Evers & Kate M. Taylor

WILLOW CREEK PRESS

Text by David C. Evers and Kate M. Taylor
Photographs © Daniel Poleschook, Jr. and Virginia R. Gumm

Published by Willow Creek Press
P.O. Box 147, Minocqua, Wisconsin 54548

Editor/Design: Andrea Donner

Library of Congress Cataloging-in-Publication Data

Evers, David C., 1962-
    Call of the loon / by David C. Evers and Kate M. Taylor.
        p. cm.
    ISBN 1-59543-390-2 (hardcover : alk. paper)
    1. Common loon. I. Taylor, Kate M., 1967- II. Title.
QL696.G33E94 2006
598.4'42--dc22

                                                        2006007569

Printed in the United States

To our children—remember to care for all that is wild in you and around you.

More than eeriness now,
I hear survival.
More than wildness,
I hear triumph.

—Jeff Fair

Acknowledgements

We thank Dr. Jim Paruk for his contribution and review of our thoughts in this book. Thank you to Darwin Long for providing insight on wintering loons. We thank Jeff Fair who has provided us invaluable historic perspective and insight for many years. Much of the information here is described in the U.S. Fish and Wildlife Service's status asssessment and conservation plan of the Common Loon (*Gavia immer*) in North America. Most of all, we extend our gratitude to the dedicated staff at the Loon Preservation Committee and BioDiversity Research Institute, to our fellow colleagues, field biologists, and the many volunteers that have been instrumental in the collection of loon data.

Table of Contents

Foreword

When I first began working with loons as a young wildlife biologist in the summer of 1978, my research vessel was a seventeen-foot canoe. For the larger lakes I would borrow whatever motor craft was available, usually a crooked aluminum derelict of one brand or another with a retired and ill-tempered two-cycle kicker bolted to its transom, a rusted tool box in the bilge containing no wrench and the wrong-sized spark plugs, and a cement-filled coffee can with no anchor line. Those were the days. My primary tools aside from the vessel and a sodden 20-pound kapok life vest, which I used for a seat cushion, were my Sears 7x35 extra wide angle binoculars, a pocket-sized notebook, and three knife-sharpened No. 2 pencil stubs. I spent a lot of time alone on the water, watching the loons. It was a good job. Didn't pay much, but I enjoyed the open sky and learned a lot.

Looking back, those really do seem like the good old days. They might also be called the Dark Ages. The body of scientific loon literature was pretty small back then. Our basic field library could be carried in a single pocket and consisted of a copy of Dr. Judith McIntyre's Ph.D. dissertation, *Biology and Behavior of the Common Loon* (printed from microfilm in small format and bound with a black cover, giving the loon biologist the look, at times, of a waterborne evangelist consulting the scriptures), and a tertiary, water-blurred photocopy of "The Common Loon in Minnesota" (Olson and Marshall, 1952—the year I was born). No one knew much about loons back then, but as I say, we were learning.

Much as I appreciate all that we learn about loons from our more complex scientific approaches these days, I'm glad that I was able to begin my work in the old-fashioned realm of naturalistic observation, simply watching objectively and getting to know the birds and their behaviors a little better, much as a good hunter knows his deer and the fisherwoman her trout. Of course, as loon science matured, the research grew more sophisticated, more complex and expensive, employing higher technologies than I cared to mess with. It was David Evers, one of the authors of this book, who discovered the technique for the regular capture of loons in order to affix different colored bracelets to their feet so that we might monitor individuals for the first time. I recognized this as a major breakthrough in our study of loon demography, toxin loading, and more—but I retained a disinclination toward handling these mysterious creatures. Plucking them out of their innocent careers, likely scaring hell out of them, and then releasing them to be forever outed seemed disrespectful, I thought.

That was 17 years ago, but even back then I realized that we had to know more—have more facts—about the loons' plight in order to fight against their disappearance, in order to conserve the species.

This was not a moral need, but rather a political one. It seemed to me then and still does today that if we know we're poisoning a system it is only sensible, logical, ethical to stop polluting it. But the world in its modern, advanced state didn't work that way. We needed scientific proof; Evers among others (including New Hampshire's Loon Preservation Committee and Kate Taylor) recognized this. And I tagged along to help, at first to judge for myself whether the capture of loons would appear abusive, but I soon observed the care with which Evers' biologists handled the birds and witnessed the immediate reuniting of pairs or families after banding. I even netted a few birds myself, and held them in my hands. But the application of higher technologies (blood and feather sampling and analysis, statistical machinations, even the small encumbrance of tarsal bands) also seemed antithetical to the loons' wild mystique. I remained skeptical.

One July night a few years ago, I

the hardware so that it could eat again. But they could use a second boat, a few more hands. The plan was to rendezvous at a remote boat landing just after dark.

Later, as our rescue flotilla motored out onto the dark lake, I thought of how many situations like this I'd seen in the early years in New Hampshire and Maine, before we had a technique to capture a loon so afflicted. How we could only watch them struggle—and how every one of them must have died an agonizing death of starvation and drowning. Now, Evers' research technique might effect a rescue, a humane and altruistic act unrelated to his scientific endeavor (or so it seemed).

Three powerful spotlight beams clicked on and we searched. Someone called out, our boat approached the victim, a loon's call played electronically now and then to attract our quarry. Closer… a net flourished, and the loon was in our custody. Under the lights of headlamps and with hemostats and wire cutters we carefully clipped off the trebles

learned another lesson. I was riding back from a good, long day of surveys on Chesuncook Lake in Maine in biologist Bill Hanson's truck with a tight, seaworthy boat in tow, when his cell phone rang. Evers' crew had observed a common loon with a fishing lure in its bill over on Wyman Lake. It was a pathetic sight, the loon appeared to be weakened and staying in one area, and they believed they might be able to capture it and remove embedded in the tongue, freed that spirit of its hideous impediment, and released it onto the black water. We sat quietly for a while out there, allowing peace to descend, and then motored back to reassemble on shore and celebrate our success in the ambient starlight.

Why do we study loons? And why another volume of answers to questions about them? I believe there is more to it than scientific or political needs for data and answers. We learn about loons because we are curious about the things we love, because knowledge leads to a deeper intimacy, a stronger connection to the object of our affection. For me, the first and primary question to any gatherer of truths is not What have you found, but rather, Why have you come here? Few wildlife biologists that I know entered their field of study in order to answer a particular scientific quandary. They come to fulfill a desire to be closer to the wilder spirits—of the wild creatures themselves, or of a chosen landscape.

And this is what brings us all together—field biologist, scientific research technician, curious reader, and interested observer—this desire for intimacy with the magic of the real world. And what the resultant inspired knowledge leads to, when shared (as in the following pages), is the opportunity for all of us together to help free the loons from entanglement in our modern web of hardware and technologies, from poisons, fishing tackle, and in the end—best of all—from the pall of misunderstanding and ignorance. And if we can do that for the loons, my God—think what we could do for ourselves.

That's what we drank to on Caratunk Landing that night as we listened to the wails of a newly unencumbered spirit out there in the starlit darkness. We weren't just celebrating the loon's revival.

We were celebrating our own.

Jeff Fair
Lazy Mountain, Alaska
February 2006

An Introduction to the Common Loon

THE COMMON LOON is a charismatic species that is a regular part of life and woodland conversations along northern lakes. Sigurd Olson, a naturalist and writer of the North Woods, once wrote of loons as a symbol of wildness that reminds us of our own connection to what remains wild in ourselves. As the space between the needs of loons and those of people cross, the loons' survival as that symbol becomes increasingly uncertain.

In the early years of loon conservation, an effort to offset impacts from human disturbance was a driving need, while the silent threat of biological pollutants was relatively unknown. The work of loons relied on affording them space; experimental use of artificial nesting islands, roping off sensitive nest sites, and coordinating chick watches for the very young. With the advent of persistent pollutants, the intersection between providing space and the necessity of a bird in the hand had arrived. Banding, sampling and tracking marked individuals not only provided a mechanism for understanding the extent and impact of biologically available contaminants, but allowed for a deeper and more

Is heaven more beautiful than the country of the muskox in summer when sometimes the mist blows over the lakes, and sometimes the water is blue, and the loons cry very often?

—Saltatha Inuit

meaningful look into loon life history. We soon learned that entire breeding populations were now at risk. Yet there is hope. As Rawson Wood, founder of the Loon Preservation Committee in New Hampshire once said, "It is the personal concern by human neighbors of the loons that makes protection possible and survival a reasonable hope." The basis for that reasonable hope lies in understanding and that is the goal of this book.

We first attempt to define what it is to be a loon; their size, age and communication, how they number and disperse around the world. What follows are questions and answers that trail a natural course through a season of a loon. Many of the answers are based on individual loons that were uniquely color-banded by biologists at BioDiversity Research Institute (BRI) in Maine and their collaborators, primarily the Loon Preservation Committee (LPC) in New Hampshire. Through tracking and observing known individuals over time, much has been added to our understanding of this species.

The last section in this book details conservation concerns and those organizations dedicated to continuing a compassionate discourse on what it means to know loons and conduct work for their survival.

How many loon species are there in the world?

THERE ARE FIVE SPECIES of loons: the Common Loon (*Gavia immer*), Yellow-billed Loon (*Gavia adamsii*), Red-throated Loon (*Gavia stellata*), Pacific Loon (*Gavia pacifica*), and Arctic Loon (*Gavia arctica*). All loon species except the Arctic Loon have relatively robust breeding populations in North America. The Yellow-billed Loon is one of North America's rarest birds. An estimated 8,000 individuals are found in northernmost North America. Its worldwide population is estimated at 16,000 individuals.

Common loons are one of 5 species of loon that are distributed throughout the northern hemisphere.

The Red-throated Loon is the widest ranging loon, while Pacific and Arctic Loons are common in the New and Old Worlds, respectively. The Seward Peninsula in Alaska is the only place in the world where all five species exist and breed.

Where is the Common Loon found and how many are there?

THE COMMON LOON is primarily a North American species (see Map 1). Only a small population of around 300 breeding pairs on Iceland can claim a non-North American status. This is a species of the North Woods and breeds across much of Canada and Alaska to the edge of the tundra zone. The vast majority of loons are found in Canada, with estimated counts estimating upwards of 94 percent of all breeding loons with over half of these being in Ontario and Quebec. Breeding populations in the United States are limited to the 14 most northerly states, including 9,000 to 13,000 adult loons in Alaska. The breeding population size in the contiguous United States is approximately 20,000 to 24,000 adult loons with the greatest densities found in Minnesota. Of these, over 2,200 territorial pairs are now found in northeastern United States, including recent expan-

Map 1. Distribution of breeding and wintering Common Loons.

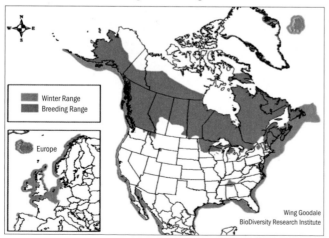

Winter Range
Breeding Range

Europe

Wing Goodale
BioDiversity Research Institute

sions into new areas of Vermont and Massachusetts. In the Great Lakes states, 6,000 to 7,300 territorial pairs occur across much of the northern regions with some isolated pairs tenuously surviving in southern and central Michigan. About 100 territorial pairs breed in western United States.

As lakes begin to ice over, many of the breeding loons are already on their ocean wintering areas. Nearly 70 percent of loons overwinter on the Atlantic Ocean, with a small group numbering approximately 4,000 individuals migrating to Western Europe. Loons wintering on the Atlantic Ocean may be found from the Canadian Maritimes south into Florida and west into the Gulf of Mexico to the Texas-Mexico border. Winter concentrations are greatest just offshore of North Carolina. The remaining 30 percent of the breeding population overwinter on the Pacific Coast, from Alaska south to Mexico's Baja Peninsula. The greatest densities are in southern British Columbia. With the creation of artificial water impoundments, such as reservoirs in Tennessee, more loons have been recorded overwintering on interior lakes. (For specific numbers of territorial pairs and adults and population trends by state and province, see Appendix 1.)

The head image of this common loon illustrates the deep red hue of their eyes.

How big is the Common Loon?

IN THE BIRD WORLD, loons are large and heavy. The Common Loon is the largest of the five species of loons. Weights vary dramatically and are dictated by migratory distance. The smallest loons are those that require long distance migratory flights between their breeding and wintering areas. For example, loons in north-central Saskatchewan have over a 1,800 mile trip to their wintering areas along the California and Mexican coastlines. Conversely, the largest individual loons, such as those found in Maine and New Hampshire, can reach their wintering areas in less than an hour's flight. These geographic pressures result in a broad range of body sizes. The smallest loons may only be 6 pounds while the largest loons can exceed 16.5 pounds—larger than any yellow-billed loon. On average, males weigh 10 to 13 pounds and females weigh 7.5 to 10 pounds.

(Below) A 13-week old chick takes flight. Strength and speed are necessary to overcome the drag of water and weight of a 7- to 13-pound loon. (Opposite) Common loons are the largest of the 5 species of loons. Weights vary between populations and are likely dictated by migratory distances.

An adult loon approaches the water's surface. Loons descend at high speeds, utilizing their webbed feet to slow and stabilize the landing. Wings are held outstretched as they slide to a stop on their abdomen.

How are loons adapted to life on water?

Loons are one of the most aquatic of bird species. Time spent on land is primarily limited to copulation and incubating. Specialized water skills are the result of physiological, morphological, and behavioral adaptations. Air is mechanically removed by compression of the air sacs and feathers allowing for quick dives. Dense bones and legs positioned far back on the body enable tremendous speed and maneuverability underwater. Most prey are regularly consumed below the water's surface, with only large or oddly-shaped items eaten above water. Unlike cormorants that must dry their feathers in the sun, loons maintain a constant waterproofing by distributing oil across their feathers. Regular maintenance of this waterproofing is essential to a loon's aquatic lifestyle.

Loons will place their head on their back and sleep for short periods.

How do loons communicate?

THE LANGUAGE OF LOONS is primarily comprised of four calls that can be translated into meaningful field interpretations. The *yodel* call is a territorial song that is only given by the male. The yodel is well studied by researchers. Until very recently, evidence indicated yodels were unique signatures of individual males. Through observations of banded males we now know that yodels may be more of a

Condensation is evident from a territorial male performing a yodel in classic yodel posture. Only males issue yodels, which are used in situations of territorial defense or threat.

signature of a territory and those individual males may alter or mimic yodel calls when changing territory. Yodels are given day and night and generally on breeding territories. The *wail* is a contact call for loons to communicate with near or far neighbors. Wails are also used between mates to locate one another. The *tremolo* call has been commonly described as the "laugh" of the loon. It is, however, more aptly described as an indicator of stress and anxiety. Tremolos are likely to be heard when a nest or chicks are threatened. It is also the only call that is used in flight to determine occupancy by other loons on a lake below. The last call is a *hoot*. This is a familial, short-range contact call among family members. Other call subtleties include a soft mewing heard between courting loons and the *peenting* of loon chicks to locate or elicit attention by their parents. Loons will also use several variations of the above calls to communicate more complex expressions. These combinations are most dramatically heard during a night chorus. On large lakes or areas with clusters of many small lakes, multiple loon pairs will regularly communicate with one another. Night chorusing is a means to check on the status of other loons within the neighborhood.

The wail call is primarily used as a contact call. Wail calls are highly variable in style, intensity, and meaning.

That night it was still, and in the moonlight the loons began as I had heard them before, first the wild, excited calling of a group of birds dashing across the water, then answers from other groups until the entire expanse of the lake was full of their music. We sat around until long after dark and listened.

—Sigurd Olson

Are males and females different?

THERE ARE NO PLUMAGE differences between male and female loons. There are, however, three key features that differentiate the sexes. First, only the male loon produces the territorial yodel call. Second, males are generally larger than females. Scientific findings from banding efforts by BRI across North America show that on average, males weigh 28 percent more than females. Third, of course, only females lay eggs. More subtle differences include a more pronounced brow line and larger bill of the male. Through patient observation, these subtleties are evident over time.

Both male and female loons incubate the eggs. Here a nest exchange begins with the approach of the mate.

How long do loons live?

LOONS ARE A RELATIVELY long-lived species. By continued tracking of loons that were banded as chicks, in time more specific loon longevity will be understood. Until then, estimations based on other loon species and species with similar life histories indicate a lifespan of 30 years. Based on banded loons, the oldest known loon is a 19-year old male banded as a chick in 1987—he is still guarding his territory at the Seney National Wildlife Refuge in Michigan. Another long-lived and relatively famous loon is the female at the Sweat Meadow territory on Lake Umbagog along the New Hampshire/ Maine border. She was banded as a breeding adult in 1993 and as of 2005, has annually returned to her lake territory.

Experienced males return first on the breeding grounds, followed by experienced females. Here, an adult loon surveys its territory as a spring snow lightly falls onto the lake.

How old is the Common Loon as a species?

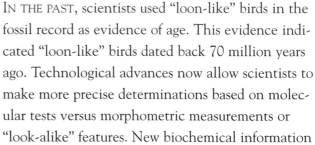

(Below) Now considered a relative, cormorants are often misidentified as common loons due to similar foraging behavior. Loons do not, however, rest on pilings or spread their wings to dry as this double-crested cormorant is doing. (Opposite) A solitary adult cares for a young chick by securing it under its wing.

IN THE PAST, scientists used "loon-like" birds in the fossil record as evidence of age. This evidence indicated "loon-like" birds dated back 70 million years ago. Technological advances now allow scientists to make more precise determinations based on molecular tests versus morphometric measurements or "look-alike" features. New biochemical information now classifies loons in a group of birds that are comparatively young and includes species such as storks, cormorants, vultures, and penguins. Modern loons are known from fossil records of 20 million years ago. Just like the myth that loons mate for life, it now appears that the idea of loons as an ancient species is just another romantic notion.

This 13-week old chick displays its white and yellow leg bands. This is an opportune time to determine if a loon has been banded, as they often display their legs above the waterline while preening.

COLOR-BANDING LOONS

Why are loons banded?

MUCH CAN BE gained by tracking known individuals. Field observations on unmarked populations have provided general knowledge; however, to more fully understand the species, marked individuals must be followed over time. Coordinated banding efforts began in 1989 by BRI. Since that time, more specific information has been discovered concerning territory fidelity, mate fidelity, initial age of breeding, dispersal within the breeding area, migratory connections, and many other life history questions.

Arise early, be quiet and listen, for the voice speaking is not our own and goes to the end of the earth.

—Thomas B. Kennedy

Discovery of a reliable and replicable method for loon capture

Capture and color-marking programs are necessary for careful studies and have been used by researchers for over 100 years. In the early years, researchers only infrequently and opportunistically banded loons. In 1989, BRI scientists discovered a replicable capture method. The ability to reliably capture targeted individuals allowed researchers to finally study the intricacies of loon natural history. Loon capture also unexpectedly provided a mechanism for not only assessing contaminants, but to later serve as a means for determining the behavioral and reproductive impacts of mercury pollution. The loon is now considered the flagship wildlife species for national mercury monitoring and policy-making.

BRI has captured and color-marked over 3,000 loons in 22 states and provinces. Loons are only captured according to justified objectives set by federal and state agencies and collaborating scientists. The capture of loons is not taken lightly; each individual loon is treated with great care and respect.

How do you catch a loon?

LOONS ARE CAPTURED at night using a combination of playback recordings and spotlights. Loons are not chased; they are instead lured to the boat where they are carefully netted. Capturing adults with young is most effective as they are more responsive to playbacks of chicks or an intruding adult. Every attempt is made to capture chicks with the adults so that family units can be released together. No loon is captured unless there is a specific research purpose or conservation need.

These colored leg bands have just been placed on the legs of a 5-week old loon chick by BioDiversity Research Institute. Leg bands provide positive identification and enable a wealth of observational data to be collected throughout a loon's life. Bands are harmless, pain-free, and do not modify the behavior of the loon.

How are loons handled and does it hurt them?

ONCE THE LOON is brought into the boat, a towel is immediately placed over the eyes. For most animals, this is a calming action. One to two people quietly hold the loon while a third quickly attends to applying bands, sampling blood and feathers and recording weight and other measurements. Blood is collected from the main leg vein and feathers are cut, not plucked. The loon suffers no pain. This process takes 15-20 minutes and upon completion, the loon is gently released back to its own territory on the lake. Follow-up observations show no obvious short-term or long-term behavior changes related to the capture and banding process. Some loons have been recaptured over five times.

A territorial adult displays orange and silver leg bands on its right leg.

How many bands are place on the leg?

The blue and red leg bands on this adult identify it in flight as a local territorial bird.

A TOTAL OF TWO to four bands are placed on each loon. Captured loons are banded for individual identification using unique combinations of color-marked bands and a numbered aluminum band. The colored bands are made of plastic and are molded to fit a loon's flattened leg. Because loon legs vary dramatically in diameter, the plastic bands are custom fit to the leg size. Although both the color and aluminum bands are long-lasting, sometimes bands end up missing. Aluminum bands wear thin over time because of saltwater. Much to the frustration of researchers, some loons have learned how to remove color bands. A female loon on a Wisconsin lake used her bill to remove her bands and kindly left them in her nest as proof. That year, along with her mate, she was recaptured and fitted with replacement color bands. The following year, she removed her bands leaving them once again on her nest. This time, her mate followed her lead leaving his leg bands on the nest as well.

What else can be gained by a bird in the hand?

THE OPPORTUNITY OF having a loon in the hand is not wasted. Samples for numerous research initiatives are gathered in addition to banding. For example, blood is taken to determine overall health and to genetically determine the relationship among individuals and populations. The cornerstone of collecting both blood and feathers is to assess contaminant levels, primarily mercury. Through this effort, loons have now become the foremost species for addressing the exposure and effects of mercury across North America.

How to observe and record color bands on a loon

Obtaining band combinations on loons is not easy. It requires patience, luck, and in time, skill. The following suggestions should prove useful in making field observations on banded birds:

1. Use a spotting scope from shore. Do not chase the birds.
2. Keep the sun at your back, look from a height of land if possible, and make observations during flat water.
3. Focus on the lower hind end of the bird. First just look for flashes of color. At a minimum this confirms that a banded individual has returned to the lake.
4. Getting the correct color band combinations is the next step. There are generally two color bands on the left leg, and for adults, the right leg has a silver-colored aluminum band that is stamped by the U.S. Fish & Wildlife Service. Many times this silver band is adjacent to a color band. It is therefore important to report the color combination and order for each leg. For example, a loon with a red band on top of a blue band on the left leg would be reported as, "left leg, red over blue."
5. Seeing the color bands is easiest during preening when the birds are most likely to foot waggle or belly preen. Generally, loons have one, 5-minute preening period every hour. Loons preen most during and just after rain.
6. Report all banded loons to BRI, 19 Flaggy Meadow Road, Gorham, Maine 04038 and the U.S. Fish and Wildlife Service Migratory Bird Office.

SEASONS OF THE LOON
Spring

IN SPRING, returning loons focus on regaining their energy stores through constant feeding forays. Particular attention is paid to feather maintenance and waterproofing. Upon arrival on the freshwater lakes, manic bouts of bathing can be observed, likely serving to remove feather mites. Wing flaps straighten and realign flight feathers after the long journey to these waters. When not feeding, loons are engaged in territorial acquisition or defending already defined ground. Because intruding loons commonly test territory holders, aggressive interactions can occur along territorial lines. It is common to see loons chasing one another underwater and wing row across the water's surface. More intense battles might find adults locking bills and beating one another with their wings. Bills can also be used to stab a foe from below. Though rare, some encounters can end in death.

*(Opposite) Wing flaps help realign flight feathers and are readily observed during preening episodes.
(Above) Engaged in territorial conflict, a loon barely evades the lunge of a challenging adult.*

What is spring migration like?

AS DAYS LENGTHEN in March, adult loons have finished their molt and have gained their breeding plumage. Overwintering individuals in the more southern part of their range begin to move singly and *en masse* north toward their breeding areas. Some individuals will gather in relatively large groups as they prepare to make their inland flight. Once in flight, loons move quickly to the northernmost open waterbody. Many individuals need to cross hundreds of miles with few open water stopover points. In these and other cases, it is important for the loon to maintain a steady 60 mph flight for 10 or more hours per day. To find their way, loons are likely visually following landscape cues. Loons only migrate during the day.

A territorial loon pair swims together amid an early spring snowfall.

How do they know their lake is ice-free?

AS THE SPRING thaw pro-
gresses, southernmost lakes
are freed up from their ice
covering sometimes weeks
in advance of more north-
ern lakes. This relatively
slow transition provides a
way for migrating loons to
stage in open, more
southerly waterbodies while
waiting for more northerly
waters to open. Loons are opportunistic while in
this migratory phase and will also regularly use
rivers. Rivers are generally free of ice before lakes
and provide opportunities for reconnaissance flights.
River-fed lakes regularly feature large groups of
loons waiting for open water.

*Loons utilize staging lakes during
spring and fall migrations. These
loons are socializing together.
Although usually solitary or paired
while breeding, socializing groups of
loons can involve several individuals.
Behaviors such as circular swimming
(circle dance), splash diving, peering,
and wing rowing can be observed.*

(Above) Yellow pond lilies are regularly found on loon lakes. (Opposite) Dense bones enhance diving abilities but can make flight difficult. Loons require a sufficient runway and speed to attain flight. On smaller lakes, it may be necessary to circle the lake in order to clear adjacent trees and mountains.

What kind of lakes do loons like?

LOONS PREFER relatively large waterbodies with clear water, suitable nesting areas, and an abundance of small fish. Breeding loons are typically found on lakes, although some will use slow-moving rivers. Acceptable lake size varies tremendously. Some loons will nest on lakes as small as 13 acres. Most loons prefer lakes that are greater than 60 acres. Two loon pairs may be present when lakes begin to approach 300 acres in size. However, shoreline configuration, presence of isolated coves, and multiple nesting islands are important predictors of increasing habitat quality for more than one pair. As lakes increase in size, the number of loon pairs increases as well. Large lakes, such as Moosehead Lake in Maine have over 50 pairs on 75,000 acres of open water. Because loons are visual predators primarily focused on fish, water clarity is essential. The way biologists measure water clarity is with a secchi disk. Secchi disk readings generally range between 6 and greater than 38 feet on lakes with nesting loons.

What is a loon territory?

This adult loon is acting defensively to a threat to its territory and/or young.

LIKE MOST BIRDS, breeding loons vocalize and protect an area on the lake that is referred to as a "territory." Loon territories can be grouped into three types: multiple-lake territories, partial lake territories, and whole lake territories. Loons that nest on small lakes (less than 60 acres) generally use more than one lake as their territory for feeding. These loons occupy what is called a multiple-lake territory. Lakes with only one pair are described as whole-lake territories. Partial lake territories are found on lakes with two or more nesting pairs. These larger lakes may also have areas that are used by non-territorial or visiting loons. In summer, around 15-20 percent of the loon populations do not hold territories and as such, they roam around hoping for an opportunity to acquire a territory from another loon.

Do they always return to the same lake?

LOONS ARE WELL KNOWN for returning year after year to their lake. Although this is true, scientific findings have shown it is not an absolute. On average, 8 out of 10 adult loons return to their previous year's territory. Some of the adults may return to the same lake but switch territories while others return to a neighboring lake instead. Rarely do territory changes involve adults moving more than 5 miles.

This photo of a loon flying in fish in northeastern Washington is the first of its kind. Loons are capable of retrieving fish from a neighboring lake and returning with it to their occupying lake. This is, however, rare and likely occurs when food is limited.

Courtship displays are minimal for loon pairs. Often, courtship simply involves synchronized bill dipping, head bobbing, and body postures. In this photo, the male is on the left; the female is on the right.

Do loons always return to the same mate?

INSTEAD OF FIDELITY to each other, loons are faithful to their territory. Territorial loons are regularly faced with challengers or intrusions on their territory by wandering loons searching for a breeding territory. These territorial challenges peak after ice-out and following a nest failure.

Information gained through tracking individual loons

1. Age for first year in breeding plumage: 2 years
2. Age at first year of breeding: 4 years
3. Longest known marked loon: 19 years (and counting)
4. Average percentage of adult loons returning to their breeding territory each year: 80%
5. Typical distance traveled when an adult leaves a breeding territory for another one: <1 to 2 miles
6. Longest known return of an individual to its same winter territory: 5 years
7. Longest known return of an individual to a breeding territory: 13 years
8. Longest known return of the same pair to the same breeding territory: 9 years

The remote spruce-edged lake shore under the cold bright moonlit spring night; a gray crust, the last remains of winter's ice, glittered along the lake's shore. Abruptly the silence was broken by loud wails, yodels, eerie cries and splashing water. It was our first signal that the loons had arrived back from their winter sojourn in the south, ready for another season.

—David Ewert

Summary

WITH TERRITORIES defined, the summer begins with the business of nesting and rearing young. Males and females share the duties of the month-long incubation and both will be engaged in caring for their chicks. Nesting loons will regularly turn the eggs to avoid the contents adhering to the sides of the shell. Loons will splay their wings and pant

This common loon is incubating 2 eggs on an island nest site. Loons nest in close proximity to the water's edge and prefer the lee side of small islands, floating bogs, and marshes. Islands provide the widest range of visibility and better protection from mammalian predators.

from the heat; however, other than short periods to cool off, the eggs are rarely left unattended. Of the many nesting postures, the most notable is the "hangover position." When threatened, the neck is lowered and extended over the nest. This has the effect of making the loon less conspicuous and readying it for a quick dive if necessary. Loon families generally stay close, softly hooting to one another. Young chicks can get chilled and are susceptible to predators and therefore regularly climb on the back of the adults. Chicks can also be "stashed" while the adults respond to an intruding loon or encroaching people. In moments of intense distress, such as when boats are too close to nest sites or young chicks, adults may "penguin dance." This posture requires a large expenditure of energy, as the loon must rise completely from the water, using its feet to run along the surface.

The "penguin dance" can be observed during times of high anxiety, especially when a nest or young chicks are threatened.

What do loons eat?

A LOON'S DIET IS largely comprised of fish. The type of fish and how many fish they eat depends on availability, season, and the size of the loon. Loons tend to prefer fish that have a zigzag escape method. For example, when confronted with a predator, a yellow perch will move from side to side as it escapes. In response, a loon will attempt to out-maneuver the perch while making quick jabs with its long neck and bill. Underwater speed is attained using the legs and webbed feet while wings are

tucked close to the body. A loon's bill has tremendous clamping strength and captured fish are swallowed underwater. Larger fish or oddly-shaped prey items such as bullheads and crayfish require swallowing above the water's surface. Scientific findings have shown that a loon family eats over 900 pounds of fish during a breeding cycle.

While fish are a staple of a loon's diet, they also feed on invertebrates such as this crayfish. Like other wild creatures, loons prefer easy and readily available prey.

Where does a loon like to nest?

LOONS GENERALLY prefer to nest along the shoreline of small islands. Some of the more favored sites are floating bog and sedge mats. Nests are constructed using surrounding materials, such as sedge, grass, moss, twigs, and mud. Some nest bowls are comprised of elaborate piles of vegetation that reach a foot in height, while others are rather simple stick and vegetation bowls. In areas with little else than sand or rock, eggs are simply laid without obvious effort of any nest construction. There are many examples of unusual nesting areas. Some of these include the tops of beaver lodges, old waterlogged docks, shorefront lawns, and rotted logs and stumps. Natural nesting areas impacted by human disturbance can be supplemented with artificial nesting islands, or "rafts."

Pictured is a loon's eye view of its surroundings at the nest site. Eggs are large and camouflaged, but vulnerable to predators if left unattended.

47

Artificial nesting islands, or "rafts," are used when natural nesting sites are unsuccessful due to excessive predation or artificial water level fluctuations that flood or strand nests.

When should artificial nesting islands be used?

RAFTS WERE FIRST used for loon pairs in the late 1970s. Since that time, they have become an effective tool for offsetting the impacts of artificial water level fluctuations that can flood nests. Rafts can also be used for nest sites that experience higher than usual rates of predation. Some predators, like raccoons, thrive in areas with shoreline development. In some situations, raft placement can fill a habitat gap that is otherwise limiting a loon pair from nesting on a lake. Rafts are an important management tool for wildlife biologists and managers, and therefore qualified individuals from loon organizations or from state and federal agencies should be consulted. Improper use of rafts can be detrimental to a nesting loon pair by attracting them to an area that has marginal or suboptimal habitat—also known as an ecological trap.

This incubating adult is in the process of turning its eggs. Eggs are turned after the adults make a nest exchange to prevent the contents from adhering to the inside shell.

Is incubation by the male or female?

THE GREAT MAJORITY of female loons lay two eggs. Nests with only one egg usually happen after the first nest has failed. The incubation period lasts from 27 to 30 days. Both the male and female will share the incubating duties equally, although there is a tendency for females to spend more time incubating than males. The longer loons incubate their eggs the greater the investment the parents have for them to hatch. Therefore, it is during the first one to two weeks that disturbance easily causes abandonment—even a thunderstorm can threaten a newly established nest. Incubation duties by the parents are usually for four to six hour stints during the day and night. This provides the non-incubating adult time to forage, preen, and in the case of males, yodel to help guard and identify his territory. Eggs are rarely left uncovered, as they are quite vulnerable to predation and overexposure to cold and heat.

Male and female loons will equally share incubation duties lasting 27-30 days.

Generally, adults will not leave their eggs unattended for more than one hour and overall an incubating adult covers eggs over 95 percent of the time. If a loon nest fails, renests occur approximately two weeks after the initial nest failure. There have been reports of three egg clutches; however these have not been confirmed from a single female.

As with incubation, both pair members will share in attending to the needs of their young.

(Above) This nesting loon is unmoved by a painted turtle seeking a warm resting place. (Opposite) Loons will defend their territories, including intrusions from other species, such as this female hooded merganser.

What are the dangers that incubating loons and their eggs face?

LOONS ARE CREATURES of the water and therefore are far more vulnerable to predators on land. Because adult loons are quite large and have formidable defense skills, few predators have the ability to predate an adult. There are examples of eagles attempting to seize incubating loons and in some cases successfully grabbing them. One of the more unusual cases of attempts to predate an incubating adult loon was on Middle Pea Porridge Pond in central New Hampshire. A lake resident awoke one morning to frantic loon calls and after searching the sources of the calls, watched as a large snapping turtle pulled an incubating loon off the nest and under water. From his canoe, he used a paddle to disrupt the turtle's grip. The freed loon surfaced and immediately returned to the nest. The biggest concern to nesting loons is egg predation. Eggs are most vulnerable when adults are flushed from the nest. Gulls, ravens and crows regularly prey upon unprotected eggs. Other nest predators include mink and raccoons. An internet-based camera by BRI documented a mink rolling loon eggs off the nest.

A male loon offers a protective wing for his newly-hatched chick.

What are the dangers that loon chicks face?

LOON CHICKS ARE small and for the first couple weeks have few defenses other than riding on their parent's back. Loon chicks must leave their nest relatively quickly as they are quite vulnerable to land and avian predators. Loon chicks are also quite buoyant during their first few days and have difficulty maneuvering. Parental protection is vital for their survival. If chicks are left unattended, birds such as the Great Black-backed Gull, Herring Gull, and Common Raven may capture a chick for food. Beneath the water, predatory fish such as northern pike and largemouth bass are a threat. Mammals will also take loon chicks. Scientists tracking loon chicks with radio telemetry have found chicks predated by fisher. However, the most notorious chick predator is the Bald Eagle. By the time loon chicks reach six weeks of age, they are much more mobile and can avoid predators with greater ease. From this point on, chick mortality is generally very low.

A territorial male engages an intruding loon in defense of his chick.

Chick Development

ONCE THE CHICKS have hatched, they will spend the next twelve weeks gaining the necessary skills for survival. There is much to learn and both adults will participate in this education. After hatching, young downy chicks are susceptible to predators and tire easily. For the first two weeks, they will seek rest and refuge by back-riding on the adults. Live prey is presented to the chicks in order to learn proper feeding skills. These meals are supplemented with other easy-to-catch items, such as crayfish and small insects. In time, more advanced skills will develop, such as capturing prey underwater, taking flight and finally a first journey to the ocean.

The following pages show a photo progression of chick development from hatch to fledge. Chick age is primarily tracked by size and feather molt patterns.

After hatch, loon chicks almost immediately leave the nest and will only infrequently return to rest.

Loon chicks are regularly fed small insects during their first days of life. Capture
of such small prey by adults exhibits tremendous bill dexterity.

A Guide for Ageing Loon Chicks

Week 1: Newly-hatched chicks have brownish-black down. Buoyancy and lack of maneuverability leave them vulnerable to predators above and below the water. Development is rapid during this time.

Week 2: Chicks are now 7 times their hatching weight and their down covering begins to appear more brown than black. Chicks at this age are more able to make shallow dives for short periods. Back riding during the first two weeks is common.

Week 3: This chick is performing a foot waggle. Foot development is rapid and disproportionate to the rest of the body. Large webbed feet are needed for improving swimming ability, aiding in food capture and evading predators. At this age, they are less than half the length of the adults and back-riding is now rare.

Week 4: At one month, loon chicks remain fully down-covered but appear more unkempt. The bill is noticeably longer at this stage.

Week 5: The first gray contour feathers begin to replace downy feathers on the upper back. Flight feathers appear along the leading edge of the wing. Most evident in this photo are the initial growth of the primary flight feathers.

Week 6: Gray contour feathers are now apparent on the back and wings. At this time, chicks are greater than half the length of the adults. Six-week old chicks have a streamlined appearance that allows for a greater ability to catch fish and escape predators.

Week 7: Now, chicks have more gray contour feathers than brown down. At this age until they fledge, there is relatively low mortality. Feeding is still being supplemented by the adults.

Week 8: Only small tufts of brown down may still be evident on the head, neck, and tail region. If food is not a limiting factor, two chicks can survive and fledge from a lake.

Week 9: At this age, loon chicks are fully covered with smooth gray contour feathers. This chick was banded one month earlier when its leg bones were large enough for adult-sized leg bands and it could be more easily captured.

Week 10: Flight feathers are now completely in and chicks will be engaged in more wing flapping and stretching behaviors.

Week 11: During their eleventh week, chicks are making take-off runs preparatory to being able to fly. Chicks will model the techniques of the adults through numerous test runs.

Week 12: Chicks are fully capable of flight at this age but rarely leave their natal lake. Although still being cared for by the adults, 12-week old chicks are able to fend for themselves. At this stage, they have nearly reached full adult size.

Week 13: Chicks are now fully capable of sustained flight and may even move to a neighboring lake.

Week 14: Once loon chicks are independent, the adults begin to leave—first one, then the other. In fall, it is common to find both siblings remaining together and fending on their own.

This banded, immature loon in winter is at a known age of nearly 2½ years. Recent, reobservations of several banded individuals show that loons attain their full breeding plumage at age two.

Fall

As FALL DRAWS NEAR, the first signs of molting are visible in the faces of the adults. They will now begin to leave their chicks for longer periods of time to gather with other adults, sometimes rafting with 100 or more individuals. Although still being cared for by the parents, the young can now fly and fend for themselves. Soon only a single adult will return to them from these gatherings and finally none. Young loons will stay longer than the more experienced adults, often lingering well into November or as long as there is open water. Soon enough the ice will force their departure and the long silence of winter will follow.

In the fall, adult loons start their molt around the base of the bill and head.

A banded female loon taking-off in the early fall. Adults will now spend more time socializing with other adults and less time with their young.

When are chicks independent?

(Above) The head of this 15-week old loon chick shows the distinctive light bill and scalloped feathers of a young of the year. (Opposite) During late summer and early fall, loon families will include one or two chicks that have grown to the size of the adults.

THE TIME WHEN loon chicks are able to fend for themselves occurs in stages. Independence actually begins soon after hatching. Unlike many hatch-lings, loon chicks are independent of their nest within 24 hours. At this age, they are able to swim, make preening motions, and most importantly, climb on the back of their parents. Although young chicks are able to regularly catch their own prey, they remain dependent on both parents to provide food for the next several weeks. As the chicks become more independent, the adults will increas-ingly spend more time socializing with other adult loons, while concurrently the chicks spend increas-ingly more time feeding themselves. Once chicks reach six weeks of age and smooth gray feathers have replaced their brown downy feathers, they are more able to forage on their own. The parents will continue to supplement the chick's diet until com-plete independence between 10 and 11 weeks. This period marks first flight attempts by the young. By week 12, these shallow practice flights have turned into actually lift-off from the lake.

During the fall, molted loon feathers can be found on lakes and ocean shorelines.

What is the molt process in fall?

LOONS EXPERIENCE a full body molt starting in late summer or early fall. The black and white breeding plumage, also known as *alternate* plumage, of the summer loons is replaced by the gray-brown of winter or *basic* plumage. The eyes of adult loons remain red year round. The onset of molt is likely dependent on changing hormones, individual age, and possibly environmental stressors. Drab gray feathers slowly replace the well-known black and white plumage of the adults. This process typically begins at the base of the bill and spreads across the head and over the upper back. The head speckling of gray replacing black seems to happen first in more northerly versus southern residents. None of the flight feathers are molted in the fall. Many times loons initiate the migration process before fully molting from the breeding plumage to the all-gray winter plumage. It is common to walk along beaches on the Great Lakes or along the ocean and find black and white loon feathers washed up to shore. By December, most loons have fully molted into their gray winter plumage.

How do loons migrate in the fall?

FALL MIGRANT LOONS take more time when moving from their breeding to wintering territory than in the spring. Some individuals start this process in late summer, but most loons leave their breeding territory between September and October. Breeding pairs and family groups do not migrate together. Many times loons migrate singly but group together on larger lakes in social gatherings called staging areas. Well-known staging areas in the U.S. include Flathead Lake, Montana, the Great Lakes, Mille Lacs, Minnesota, and Walker Lake, Nevada. Overland migration altitude can reach over 1.5 miles while loons migrating over water are usually within 100 feet or less of the surface. Loons are visual migrants likely using landmarks such as mountain chains, coastlines, and large rivers to guide them during their daytime treks.

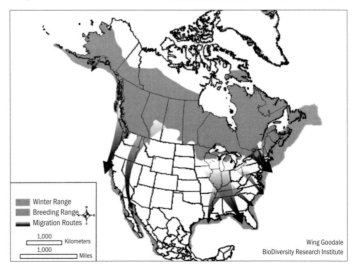

Map 2. Migratory connections between breeding and wintering populations based on reobservations of banded individuals.

Winter Range
Breeding Range
Migration Routes

1,000 Kilometers
1,000 Miles

Wing Goodale
BioDiversity Research Institute

71

Winter

AS THE BREEDING grounds lay frozen in wait, the coastal wintering waters welcome back the adults as well as the new generation. Although a small number of two-year olds will migrate back to the breeding grounds, most young of the year will stay now, usually for three years, before returning to their natal area. With the duties of breeding past, time here is spent foraging in loose flocks or alone and rafting together at night. Loons are more tolerant of other birds during these winter months and will mingle with other species. Infrequent calling is used to keep in contact. Preening becomes a vigilant duty, especially as the winter molt progresses.

A young, over wintering loon is shown during an active preening bout.

What physiological changes occur when moving from freshwater breeding areas to marine wintering areas?

LOONS SPEND JUST as much of their lives at sea as on their breeding lakes. This split lifestyle requires an ability to manage both fresh and saline environments. Birds generally manage the excess salt of marine habitats by utilizing a specially adapted salt gland. This gland concentrates a salty solution that will eventually exit through the bird's nares (or nostrils). This gland is under hormonal control and is activated when the loon enters saltwater environments.

On the ocean, excess salt is eliminated through the nares (nostrils).

What is typical wintering habitat and do loons return to the same wintering locations?

WINTERING LOONS are mostly found along inland coastal waters including channels, coves, and bays as opposed to deeper water locations. Other research has shown marine locations are based on prey availability which is dictated by salinity gradients, clarity, tides, and depth. Based on loons banded by BRI, recent scientific findings indicate that loons indeed return to the same area each winter. This is similar to other bird species. A female banded on Stillwater Reservoir in Montana has been repeatedly observed in Morro Bay, California, most every winter from December 2000 to March 2006.

Commercial fish netting activities pose a serious threat to wintering loons.

Do loons call during the winter?

LOONS DO VOCALIZE in the winter, though to a lesser extent. Hoots and short wails are most commonly heard when loons are in close contact with each other, such as in feeding flocks or rafting together at night. These vocalizations allow for the group to maintain contact. As on summering locations, tremolos are given when stressed. Territorial yodel calls are rarely heard.

This winter-plumaged adult is in the initial stages of molting into breeding plumage. Note the black feathers at the base of the bill.

What do loons eat in the winter?

DAILY ACTIVITIES ON the wintering grounds center around feeding, with loons employing one of two foraging strategies: 1) flock-feeding on schools of fish, such as menhaden or gulf silversides, or 2) solitary feeding where prey items are more evenly dispersed. Inshore larger prey, such as crabs and flounder, are ingested above water.

This adult common loon in basic (winter) plumage is feeding on a kelp crab. Crabs are eaten by breaking off the legs and swallowing the carapace.

(Right) A wing flap reveals the final stages of the molt process occurring after arrival to the wintering grounds. This adult is missing several primary and secondary flight feathers that will leave it flightless for a 2-week period. (Opposite) An adult common loon in full breeding plumage.

What molting process do loons undergo in winter?

BETWEEN LATE December and April, adults undergo a complete molt of their flight feathers. This molt causes loons to be flightless for a period of two to three weeks until all flight feathers are regrown. By mid-April, loons have molted back into breeding plumage and begin migrating back to their traditional freshwater breeding grounds.

A fishing leader and swivel can be seen dangling from the bill of this loon. Annual mortality from ingestion of lead fishing tackle, entanglement in fishing line or nets is significant. It is also avoidable.

LOON CONSERVATION

What are the threats to loon survival?

THE SURVIVAL of the loon hinges on our ability to
lessen the impacts to human disturbance. On the
breeding grounds, the loss of nesting habitat from
shoreline development is occurring at a rapid pace.
Shallow nesting areas are now more readily accessi-
ble to recreational activity. Nests washed out from
the wake of personal watercraft or incubating loons
flushed from nests by canoes and kayaks impact
hatching success. Strikes from speeding boats pose a
serious threat to the survivorship of adults and their
young in open water. Ingestion of lead
tackle and monofilament entanglement
continues to cause avoidable mortality.
New scientific findings link atmospheric
mercury deposition from coal-burning
facilities and reduced reproductive
success—thus having the ability to impact
entire breeding populations. Wintering
loons, flightless for a period during the
winter molt, are susceptible to oil spills,
red tide and emaciation syndrome.

*A loon inspects a Styrofoam cup
carelessly discarded on the lake.*

CASE STUDY: What happens when a loon swallows a lead sinker?

IN THE NORTHEAST, lead poisoning from ingested fishing tackle is the leading cause of death to adult loons. Lead affects nerve impulse transmission causing slow, systemic paralysis and neurological dysfunction. In the early stages, lead poisoned loons will exhibit behaviors such as head shaking,

This angler has unknowingly maneuvered into position very near a loon's nest. Increased recreational activity and shoreline development have been implicated in reduced reproductive success.

gaping, and disorientation. Affected loons appear lethargic; often remaining in shallow areas where less nutritious food sources such as crayfish, are readily captured. Frequent bouts of beaching occur as the condition progresses. Lead poisoning eventually leads to death, often within two weeks of ingestion or within a week of the initial field symptoms. There is no treatment for lead poisoned loons.

In studies by the LPC and Tufts University Wildlife Clinic in Massachusetts, mortality from lead peaks mid-summer at a time of peak tourism and angling pressure. Weakened fish trailing hook, line, and sinker are an easy source of prey for a loon. The presence of swivels and hooks in close to half of the lead-killed loons suggest that this mode of ingestion, rather than the reservoir of lost tackle on lake bottoms, is the primary source of continuing mortality.

Loons and Lead Are a Deadly Mix

On July 4, 1999, LPC biologists were called to Lovell Lake in central New Hampshire to capture a sick loon. This lake had a long history of loons successfully rearing young in a unique and secluded nest site. Accessing the nest required swimming under a low bridge that separated the nest site from the lake proper. Each year the young, when old enough to travel on the greater lake, had to be taught to swim under this bridge. When the sick loon was brought to a veterinarian, a radiograph showed the presence of a lead jig head. The loon, the female of the pair, was humanely euthanized. By noon the following day, the male loon was found dead, sharing the same fate as his mate. Within 24 hours, the Lovell Lake pair was lost from lead poisoning and with them, the memory of their unique nesting area.

CASE STUDY: What happens when a loon gets too much mercury in its diet?

MERCURY IS A natural element that fulfills no biological requirement in a loon. Although loons have evolved with a certain amount of mercury in the ecosystem, more mercury has been distributed and mobilized in the environment in recent history. Once the inorganic mercury is converted to the much more toxic methylmercury form, the magnification of mercury within the foodweb can quickly reach toxic levels. Loons do have natural defense mechanisms to rid their bodies of the mercury. They can bind much of it in their feathers and store it in the liver and kidney. However, if too much mercury is in the fish that the loons eat, mercury will accumulate within the loon's body. As such, older individuals will be at greater risk than younger ones.

Atmospheric deposition of mercury and acid rain impact loon health and productivity.

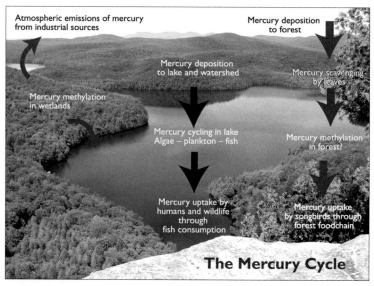

Atmospheric emissions of mercury from industrial sources

Mercury deposition to forest

Mercury deposition to lake and watershed

Mercury scavenging by leaves

Mercury methylation in wetlands

Mercury cycling in lake
Algae – plankton – fish

Mercury methylation in forest?

Mercury uptake by humans and wildlife through fish consumption

Mercury uptake by songbirds through forest foodchain

The Mercury Cycle

Recent findings in New England demonstrate that if mercury input to a loon exceeds its ability to get rid of it, individuals can accumulate mercury at an average rate of 10 percent per year. Loons with a mercury body burden greater than what evolution has allowed will be poisoned. Loons with high levels of mercury are more lethargic, less likely to incubate eggs, and have lower success in fledgling young.

Loons as Indicators of Mercury Poisoning

In August of 1999, BRI and LPC biologists banded a female loon on Swains Lake in New Hampshire. Six months later, lab results from a sample of her blood uncovered what the biologists had been suspecting; the Swains Lake loons were severely contaminated with mercury. The level of mercury, however, was so high that it necessitated further research by both groups and their collaborators, including the U.S. Fish and Wildlife Service. Subsequent studies on Swains Lake and loons on nearby lakes confirmed that this female contained some of the highest blood mercury levels in North America—a comparison based on over 3,000 loons with known mercury levels. The question soon became "why here?"

A comparison with mercury deposition models produced by the U.S. Environmental Protection Agency provided the clues. A high concentration of city incinerators and coal-burning facilities in southern New Hampshire and eastern Massachusetts were the likely culprits. These types of facilities are well known sources of atmospheric mercury. Several were within 100 miles upwind of Swains Lake. The Swains Lake female helped persuade state and regional legislators to reduce mercury emissions for the area, which has now become known as a biological mercury hotspot.

In December 2005, the Swains Lake female was found dead on the very shore that she spent the past six years attempting to hatch her eggs. Of the laid 11 eggs she produced during that time, only four hatched. As a testament to her plight, the New Hampshire legislature has been attempting to better regulate mercury emissions with positive results. Already, mercury levels found in loons in the affected area are approaching healthier levels. These efforts have created a greater understanding of the relationship between loons and lakes; if loons are healthy, so too are the lakes they live upon.

Ferry Lake Male, Washington

By Daniel Poleschook, Jr. and Virginia R. Gumm

OCTOBER 28, 2005, was the end of the life of a well-studied and frequently observed adult male common loon. His body was recovered on the shoreline of Puget Sound near Shine, Washington.

From 1999 through 2005, this loon held territory on Ferry Lake, Washington. Despite challenges and adversity, he defended his territory, producing 14 eggs resulting in nine fledglings—great accomplishments in the loon world.

Of all the common loons that have been studied thus far in the Pacific Northwest, the Ferry Lake male unknowingly provided the greatest amount of observational and photographic data that will be used for future common loon conservation in the region. His activity was documented in several studies funded by the United States Forest Service and helped determine food requirements and feeding disruptions of loon chicks at their natal lake.

No longer will the Ferry Lake male fly off on short early-morning reconnaissance flights, his calls echoing between the mountains of the Okanogan Highlands. He will no longer provide protection to

No one who has ever heard the diver's music—the mournful far-carrying callnotes and the uninhibited, cacophonous, crazy laughter—can ever forget it.

—Oliver Austin

young chicks. He will not dive the depths of Ferry Lake, Puget Sound, or waters in between. His legacy and his surviving fledglings live on.

The Ferry Lake male protects two young chicks in Washington, June 2004. From 1999-2005, he reared 9 fledglings.

What can you do?

Become a member. There are numerous organizations across the country dedicated to loon conservation (please see appendix II for a summary list). Many of these organizations need volunteers to assist in their efforts such as participating in censuses, monitoring nest sites, and collecting reproductive data.

Become a steward. Participate with local lake associations to encourage responsible fishing practices, such as the use of non-lead tackle, low-impact shoreline development, and responsible recreational activities. Create an awareness and appreciation for lake wildlife and areas that serve as nesting habitat.

Get involved. Larger issues, such as mercury, require regulations that reduce use and emissions. Support legislation that improves efforts by local, state, and federal entities to better regulate pollution.

What we do to the animals we do to ourselves.

—Rachel Carson

Why should I care about loons?

LOONS HAVE BECOME the signature species for understanding environmental quality. Legislative changes to mercury and lead laws have primarily been based on research done on banded loon populations. As a highly charismatic species, these recent strides have had much public attention and support. The importance of loons, however, is much older than the science. For many of us, a starry night and a chorus of loons is both nourishment and respite. To care about loons is to fully know we are less without their companionship.

A thing is right when it tends to preserve the integrity, stability, and beauty of the biotic community. It is wrong when it tends otherwise."

—Aldo Leopold

Appendix 1. Estimated population and trends of the common loon.

REGION	Est. # of territorial pairs	Estimated # of adults	Population trend
UNITED STATES	11,704 - 15,180	29,827 - 36,911	
Alaska	3,600 - 6,000	8,890 - 13,200	Stable
Idaho	3	10	Stable
Maine	1,700	4,100	Stable
Massachusetts	20	48	Increasing
Michigan	416	1,500	Stable/Decreasing
Minnesota	4,142 - 5,159	10,355 - 12,897	Stable
Montana	60 - 65	160	Stable/Decreasing
New Hampshire	199	515	Stable
New York	216 - 270	804 - 1,036	Increasing
North Dakota	14	48	Decreasing
Vermont	48	135	Increasing
Washington	12	38	Decreasing
Wisconsin	1,250	3,131	Stable
Wyoming	24	58	Stable
CANADA	242,075 - 244,575	581,096 - 587,096	
Alberta	1,000	2,400	Stable
British Columbia	25,000	60,000	Stable
Manitoba	10,000 - 12,000	24,000 - 28,800	Stable
New Brunswick	1,174	2,934	Stable
Newfoundland	5,000	12,000	Stable
Northwest Territories	45,000	108,000	Stable
Nova Scotia	1,200	2,880	Decreasing
Nunavut	5,000	12,000	Stable
Ontario	97,000	232,800	Stable
Quebec	50,000	120,000	Stable
Prince Edward Island	1	2	Stable
Saskatchewan	1,500 - 2,000	3,600 - 4,800	Stable
Yukon	200	480	Stable
ICELAND	300	720	Stable
GREENLAND	200 - 2,000	480 - 4,800	Stable
TOTAL POPULATION	254,279 - 262,055	612,123 - 629,527	

Appendix II. Organizations of interest for loon conservation

Alaska

Anchorage Audubon: www.anchorageaudubon.org

Alaska Loon Watch:
members.aol.com/djl4loons/loonorgs

California

Morro Bay Audubon: www.morrocoastaudubon.org

Canada

Bird Studies Canada of the Canadian Lakes Loon Survey
www.bsc-eoc.org

Maine

BioDiversity Research Institute
The International Center for Loon Conservation
Northeast Loon Study Working Group
International Loon/Diver Working Group
www.briloon.org

Maine Audubon Society: www.maineaudubon.org

Massachusetts

Massachusetts Aquatic Conservation Society
www.macsloon.org

Tufts University Wildlife Clinic
www.tufts.edu.

Massachusetts Department of Fish & Game
www.mass.gov

Department of Conservation and Recreation
www.mass.gov/dcr

Michigan

Michigan Loon Preservation Association
www.michiganloons.org

Minnesota

Journey North: www.learner.org/jnorth

Minnesota Dept of Natural Resources
www.dnr.state.mn.us

Montana

Montana Loon Society: www.montanaloons.org

New Hampshire

Loon Preservation Committee: www.loon.org

New York

Adirondack Cooperative Loon Program
www. adkscience.org/loons

Audubon International, Loon Project
www.audubonintl.org

Vermont

Vermont Institute of Natural Sciences: www.vinsweb.org

Wisconsin

Sigurd Olsen Environmental Institute, Loon Watch
www.northland.edu/soei

Washington

Loon Lake Loon Association
www.loons.org

About the Photographers
Daniel Poleschook, Jr. and Virginia (Ginger) R. Gumm

Ginger and Daniel have been nature photographers since the early 1970s, and have photographed as a team since 1992. Since 1996 they have specialized in capturing images of common loons and other water birds while conducting research and doing conservation work on common loons in the Pacific Northwest. Along with their conservation work, Daniel operates Daniel Poleschook Nature Photography and the Loon Lake Wildlife Gallery in Loon Lake, Washington. These companies specialize in publishing nature images and selling large, limited-edition prints of wildlife, specializing in water birds and featuring the common loon as their signature species. Daniel and Ginger's mission is to observe, document, and record the behavior and ecology of common loons, and to coordinate conservation efforts for common loons and other water birds. All of their compositions are authentic; they do not derive or contrive compositions nor photograph at game farms or zoos. They present their images herein hoping that viewers will gain a better understanding of the common loon and the conservation it requires, and also the important part everyone plays in preserving the environment.

About the Authors
David C. Evers and Kate M. Taylor

Dr. David Evers is the Executive Director, Founder and Senior Scientist for BioDiversity Research Institute, an ecologically-minded nonprofit based in Gorham, Maine. BRI conducts original research and monitoring projects across North America with an emphasis on using loons as indicators of aquatic integrity. Evers has actively conducted loon research for 20 years. He resides in Standish, Maine, with his wife, Kate.

Kate Taylor is Senior Biologist for the Loon Preservation Committee (LPC) and has overseen the scientific program since 1996. LPC monitors every known nesting pair of loons in the state and continues to assess population status and breeding success on a yearly basis. Taylor has actively conducted loon research for 11 years and resides in Standish, Maine, with her husband, Dave.

About the DVD

The DVD included with this book is made possible through the generosity of BioDiversity Research Institute (BRI), in Gorham, Maine. BioDiversity is a leader in loon conservation efforts throughout North America. For more information, or to make a donation to support their work, visit their website at www.briloon.org. Be sure to check out Adopt A Loon. It's a fun and unique way you can help support loon conservations efforts.

In 2003, loon researchers from BRI were the first to capture remote, live video images of nesting common loons. Using a robotic camera powered by solar panels, this fascinating project enabled scientists to monitor a nesting pair of loons without disturbing them. Special equipment that incorporated the use of infrared technology allowed 24 hour observation, even under the cover of darkness. The live video can be viewed over the internet, by the public, during the nesting season, which is typically May and June. Be sure to check the website: www.briloon.org and click on the education tab.

BioDiversity hopes to produce a full length documentary DVD using footage from the first three seasons of the live loon webcam. Proceeds from the sale of these DVDs will help fund conservation efforts involving common loons. If you enjoyed the DVD included with this book, you will want to purchase the feature length documentary version to follow. Please check the website— www.briloon.org—frequently for news about when the DVD will be released.